In the

This book belongs to

_____

Written by Stephen Barnett
Illustrated by Rosie Brooks

Contents

In the garden 3

When I grow up 13

Clouds and sunshine.................................... 21

New words 31

What did you learn? 32

About this book

Repetition of words along with rhyming will catch the interest of the reader and encourage him or her in learning new words to expand their knowledge. Readers will enjoy the stories again and again.

In the garden

I am in the garden with my mother and father.

It is Spring. We want to grow flowers in the garden.

First we put
the seeds in the soil.

Then we put some soil over the seeds.

Now we water the seeds.

We wait for the new plants to come up.

Soon
the little plants are big.

The flowers are
pretty and full of colour.

I like to be
in the garden.

When I grow up

When I grow up, I will

sail on the sea.

When I grow up, I will

go into space.

When you grow up,
come with me

into space and
out on the sea.

When we grow up,
this is where we will be!

Clouds and sunshine

I like it when it rains. I can play in puddles.

I like it when the sun shines. We can kick the ball.

When it is windy
we can fly kites,

and lie on the grass and
watch the clouds go by.

When there is a storm
then I stay inside.

If it is very hot then
I sit under the tree.

Some days
there is everything!

There are clouds
and sunshine,

wind and rain,
all in one day!

New words

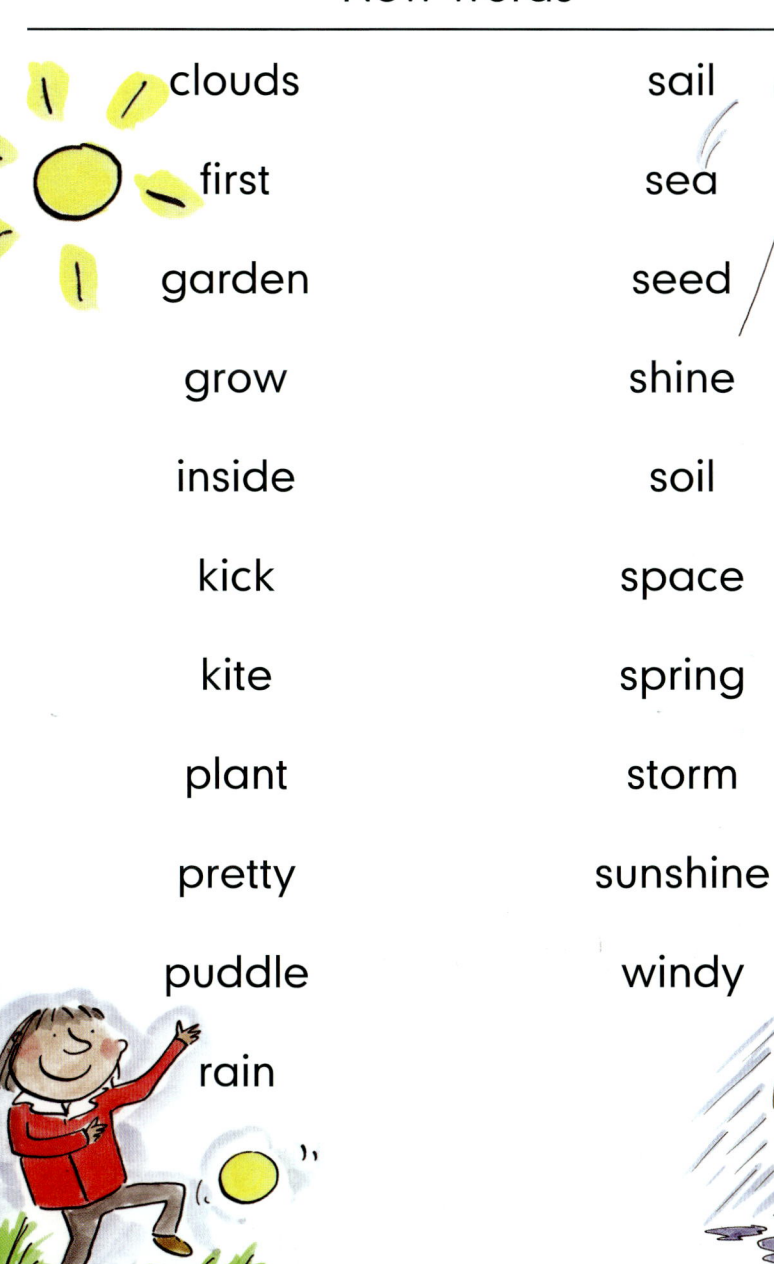

clouds	sail
first	sea
garden	seed
grow	shine
inside	soil
kick	space
kite	spring
plant	storm
pretty	sunshine
puddle	windy
rain	

What did you learn?

In the garden
What are they growing in the garden?
What is the colour of the flowers?

When I grow up
What is the colour of the rocket ship?
How many windows does the rocket ship have?
What can the boy see in space?

Clouds or sunshine
What do the children do on windy days?
What do the children do on rainy days?
What happens when there is a storm?